Security Leader Insights for Information Protection

Security Leader Insights for Information Protection

Lessons and Strategies from Leading Security Professionals

Bob Fahy, Contributing Editor

ELSEVIER

AMSTERDAM · BOSTON · HEIDELBERG · LONDON
NEW YORK · OXFORD · PARIS · SAN DIEGO
SAN FRANCISCO · SINGAPORE · SYDNEY · TOKYO

Security
Executive Council

Elsevier
225 Wyman Street, Waltham, MA 02451, USA
The Boulevard, Langford Lane, Kidlington, Oxford, OX5 1GB, UK

Notices
Knowledge and best practice in this field are constantly changing. As new research and experience broaden our understanding, changes in research methods, professional practices, or medical treatment may become necessary.

Practitioners and researchers must always rely on their own experience and knowledge in evaluating and using any information, methods, compounds, or experiments described herein. In using such information or methods they should be mindful of their own safety and the safety of others, including parties for whom they have a professional responsibility.

To the fullest extent of the law, neither the Publisher nor the authors, contributors, or editors, assume any liability for any injury and/or damage to persons or property as a matter of products liability, negligence or otherwise, or from any use or operation of any methods, products, instructions, or ideas contained in the material herein.

Library of Congress Cataloging-in-Publication Data
A catalog record for this book is available from the Library of Congress

British Library Cataloguing-in-Publication Data
A catalogue record for this book is available from the British Library

ISBN: 978-0-12-800843-0

For more publications in the Elsevier Risk Management and Security Collection, visit our website at **store.elsevier.com/SecurityExecutiveCouncil**

This book has been manufactured using Print On Demand technology. Each copy is produced to order and is limited to black ink. The online version of this book will show color figures where appropriate.

ELSEVIER Book Aid International Working together to grow libraries in developing countries

www.elsevier.com • www.bookaid.org

CONTENTS

PART 1 STRATEGIES FOR COLLABORATION BETWEEN CORPORATE AND INFORMATION SECURITY

Learn how security can benefit from existing information technology policies and explore new security and information technology collaborations.

By Ray Bernard, president and principal consultant for Ray Bernard Consulting Services, a group of expert security management and technology consultants; and subject matter expert faculty member, Security Executive Council.

Forget the dated and ineffective term "convergence" and move to clearer ways of describing how to bring business units and technologies together to better address and manage risk.

With insight from Dave Kent, vice president of Global Risk and Business Resources for Genzyme and a member of the Board of Advisors of the Security Executive Council; Terry Neely, President of PlaSec Inc.; and John McClurg, vice president of Honeywell Global Security and a member of the Board of Advisors of the Security Executive Council.

Learn how to develop a positive relationship between corporate security and information security with these suggestions from experienced security professionals.

With insight from Lou Magnotti, chief information officer, U.S. House of Representatives; Liz Lancaster, director of member services, Security Executive Council; Lorna Koppel, vice president and chief information security officer, Iron Mountain; and John Masserini, information security officer, Dow Jones & Co.

PART 2 EMERGING ISSUES IN INFORMATION PROTECTION

(ISC)², Louis Magnotti, CIO for the U.S. House of Representatives; and William Crowell, former deputy director of the National Security Agency, current chairman of the Senior Advisory Board to the Director of National Intelligence, and a member of the Security Executive Council's Board of Advisors.

Demystify the Federal Rules of Civil Procedure (FRCP) and learn how to protect your company's electronically stored information with these steps for compliance.

By William Plante, director of professional services for Aronson Security Group, based in Seattle.

INTRODUCTION

In early 2014, Hewlett-Packard published its annual Security Research Cyber Risk Report, which identified the common types of vulnerabilities companies faced in 2013. The conclusions in this year's report were alarming, to say the least. Despite all the recent attempts at improving information protection, the following bleak statistics pervaded:

- *56% of the applications tested exhibited weaknesses in revealing information about the application, its implementation, or its users.*
- *74% of the applications exhibited unnecessary permissions.*
- *80% of the applications were vulnerable to misconfiguration vulnerabilities.*
- *Hybrid development frameworks for mobile applications didn't address many well-known security issues.*[1]

As security professionals, what can we do to combat growing cybersecurity threats within our organizations and national critical infrastructure? How can we find a balance between fulfilling our businesses' need for technology and applications and our responsibility to protect our most valued information and assets? There is no easy answer to either of these two questions. However, we can look to the experiences of our peers to find shared strategies and possible solutions for the management of our information.

In *Security Leader Insights for Information Protection*, we have tapped some of the industry's most distinguished security professionals for their opinions and expertise on security's role in information protection.[2] This collection of timeless best practices is a quick and effective way to bring staff and/or contractors up to speed on topics related to the convergence of corporate and IT security, emerging issues, and information protection regulations and standards. The short, straight-to-the-point chapters provide the reader with an easily accessible

---

[1]"Report examines complete attack surface," Hewlett-Packard, accessed March 25, 2014, http://info.hpenterprisesecurity.com/register_hpenterprisesecurity_cyber_risk_report_2013.
[2]Please note that the security practitioners who contributed to these articles may no longer be at the companies listed at the time this book is published.

overview of current issues in information protection. In the event you are forced to make rapid, significant change within your business or organization, this resource can help guide transformational change. Instead of reinventing the wheel when faced with a new challenge, these proven practices and principles will allow you to execute with confidence knowing that your peers have done so with success.

Bob Fahy
Director of Corporate Security, Kraft Foods

PART 1

Strategies for Collaboration between Corporate and Information Security

CHAPTER 1

Security and Information Technology Alignment

By Ray Bernard, president and principal consultant for Ray Bernard Consulting Services, a group of expert security management and technology consultants; and subject matter expert faculty member, Security Executive Council.

In the consulting work that my colleagues and I do, we almost always find simple steps that corporate and physical security departments can take to better align themselves with information technology (IT). However, I recently realized that it is wrong to think of IT policies and practices as "rules to follow" or "hoops to jump through"—phrasing them this way conceals an important point: IT policies and practices are what company management has approved and mandated for security and cost-effectiveness reasons.

Applying the IT policies to your physical security technology means improving how you do things for your department and your overall organization's benefit. That's what the following question and answer relate to:

Q: I have been reading about the importance of aligning our security department with the IT department; but, since we don't have any ongoing or upcoming technology projects, I don't know whom to talk to about what. Are there any common starting points for such discussions?

A: There definitely are, and once you get collaboration going, you will find plenty of common ground.

IT departments have been dealing with computer and network technology for decades, and have learned—often the hard way—how to manage technology deployments and take care of the technology in place to get the maximum performance with minimum effort and cost. Using their policies can help you get more for your technology money, and help you obtain beneficial resources from outside your department—essentially they get more results with less effort. A good starting point is to find relevant IT policy documents and figure out how they can apply to electronic security systems and the data they generate.

Typically, each policy will spell out to whom the document applies and the roles, responsibilities, rights, and privileges involved, along with any specific requirements. Usually, the document contains a glossary clarifying exactly what IT means by a particular word or phrase—that data alone is valuable.

IT departments have become much more adept than most security departments at managing technology and ensuring that it performs the way it needs to and managing enterprise-scale deployments in a cost-effective manner. This is because they have so much critical technology to deal with, and almost all of it is enterprise-wide in its use. This can make outage impacts enterprise-wide, having a much greater impact than, for example, a single card reader failing. This doesn't mean IT never has problems, but it does mean that they minimize the number and impact of problems that might occur.

The cost-effective aspect of technology deployment is an area where security can usually make improvements. For example, many security departments don't have up-to-date as-built drawings for its systems. As a result, troubleshooting and repairs take longer and cost more than they should. Planning technology changes (not rip-and-replace) is more trouble and takes more time, because all the information needed is not readily at hand.

Electronic physical security systems are classified as critical systems (if yours are not, they should be!). Thus, there is an IT policy that can help improve technology deployments; in fact, there is usually at least one policy that actually makes it a company requirement to have updated as-builts, backups of system and device configurations, and so on. This IT policy is typically called configuration management or production change control. It includes keeping good records for and good control over what systems are in production use, and how to plan and manage updates and upgrades. Typically, correct application of this company policy will beneficially impact system documentation, maintenance contracts with service providers, and the planning and execution of technology updates and upgrades—all in the direction of making security technology deployments less troublesome and more cost-effective.

Try locating your IT department's configuration management policy, and find out how security can benefit by getting compliant with this existing company policy. IT can help you do this, and when initial costs are involved, IT can provide business-case support because they already know these practices save money in the long run. That's one reason such practices are company policy.

For the IT folks, it would be a welcome change to have an individual business function such as security approach them to learn about their policies and ask for help in getting compliant. It is one way to start security/IT collaborations off on the right foot.

There are often a dozen categories of IT policy, standards, practices, and procedures that apply to physical security departments and their systems technology. They can include how to use network resources, password policies, procurement practices, pilot testing, asset management, maintenance policies and lifecycle planning, compliance, and more.

CHAPTER 2

Moving Beyond Convergence

With insight from Dave Kent, vice president of Global Risk and Business Resources for Genzyme and a member of the Board of Advisors of the Security Executive Council; Terry Neely, President of PlaSec Inc.; and John McClurg, vice president of Honeywell Global Security and a member of the Board of Advisors of the Security Executive Council.

Since the early 2000s, it seems that every industry manufacturer, magazine, and communiqué has been bandying the term "convergence" about like a puck in a hockey rink. Is anyone else tired of it? This is certainly not to say that the concepts that make up convergence aren't wise and shouldn't be incorporated in some way into every security program. But I'm convinced that the way we talk about those concepts is helping to hamper their growth and adoption. Let's start with three reasons to strike convergence out of our vocabulary.

1. **We don't know what it means.** Convergence is no longer a new term. The fact that it has to be constantly defined, even in writings and seminars within our own industry, is not a good sign. "We used convergence early on," said Dave Kent, vice president of Global Risk and Business Resources for Genzyme and a member of the Board of Advisors of the Security Executive Council. "We started bringing together physical and IT security in the late 1990s, when convergence was the leading edge. There seems to be less clarity around it now than there was back then. It has gone from this grand idea of tying together risk-related functions to 'Do your physical systems reside on the IT backbone?' at the lowest level."

   Language exists to communicate meaning. If we can't decide on a meaning for a word after all this time, maybe we should pack it up and retire the word. There are other terms that more narrowly and, perhaps, more accurately describe the various elements that different people equate with convergence. For instance, Terry Neely, President of PlaSec Inc., found "systems interoperability" and "systems collaboration" helpful phrases to describe physical security systems' cooperation with the other systems on the IT apparatus.

Dave Kent referred to the organizational side of convergence—that is, the merging of the physical and information security business functions, as well as other functions in many cases, under common leadership—as a "unified model" of management.

Yes, these terms may need to be defined on occasion as well, but at least you know right away whether you're talking about technology or business structure. Surely that's a step up.

2. **It implies a singular "rightness."** Industry bloggers, experts, and watchers have been known to deride some security programs or technology implementations as employing less than "true convergence." The word's abstractness (see #1) appears to lend it a sense of superiority; the idea is that convergence is a very hard-won thing, like the Holy Grail of security, and if you don't do it just so, then it isn't really convergence. However, due to the inherent differences in security programs and the businesses they protect, there is no such thing as true convergence, and neither should there be.

What works well in one company or with one set of systems or infrastructure may not work at all in another, said John McClurg, vice president of Honeywell Global Security and a member of the Board of Advisors of the Security Executive Council: "Converged organizations come in all shapes and sizes and with varying degrees of seamlessness." Rather than one correct "converged" model, he said, "it's more of a spectrum across which various organizations can distribute themselves in a converged world. Notwithstanding the temptation we often struggle with to see something as an exact science, this truly is an art. And art is that about which rational minds can and do differ."

3. **It doesn't speak to management.** "Here's what best describes our program," said Genzyme's Dave Kent: "It's a business security program, with an emphasis on risk as it relates to people, information, and products that are brought in contact with risk through global operations." "Risk" is what corporate management and the board of directors are interested in.

In most cases, convergence doesn't convey that focus. When it is defined for management (see #1), here's what they'll hear: "We want to combine business units (*friction, tension, change*) and our IT and physical security technology (*expense, interruption, hassle*)." Convergence puts the focus on change, cost, discomfort, and pushing two things together. And since you have to define it before you can talk about its benefits, all those negative connotations will be right up front to block the view of any business value you go on to propose.

It's hard to win talking about convergence. It's more effective to talk about risk. You want to reduce a duplication of effort and cost among various business units. You want to ensure greater protection of intellectual property and physical assets by managing risk in a holistic manner, combining physical and logical security technology and staff to accomplish better security. You want to improve information sharing between functions to better enable the identification of untapped efficiencies. That's what speaks to management.

The thrust of all this is that convergence has become an ineffective word that unintentionally slanders some truly game-changing ideas. Bringing business units and technologies together to better address and manage risk is not only smart but necessary, and it's a move from which many organizations have gleaned spectacular results.

Watch Your Language

Instead of using "convergence," consider these other terms:

For the combining or collaboration of functional roles and management structure:
Unified Risk Oversight™
Unified model of management

For the ability of physical access control systems (and others) to collaborate with the rest of the IT security apparatus:
Systems interoperability
Systems collaboration

While these terms may also need defining now and again, they are clearer than convergence and they shift the focus from change and cost to risk and opportunity.

INTERLINKED THREATS ARE NOT BEST ADDRESSED IN SILOS

In Honeywell's 2007 benchmarking study "Enterprise Threat Management and Security Convergence," only 30 percent of respondents claimed to have seen an interlinked breach—a physical security breach causing an IT security threat, or vice versa. However, nearly 73 percent of respondents believe vulnerability to such breaches exists. Honeywell's McClurg easily related examples of interlinked threats.

"In the early days when hacking and phreaking were just emerging as threats that the IT community was concerned with, I had occasion to go up against a phreaker who, with a rather unsophisticated pick set, had breached the 30-year-old locks on the doors of central offices of the phone company," said McClurg, who ran security for a major communications company prior to joining Honeywell. "With that set he opened up the door into a realm in which he gathered passwords, equipment, and other things that enabled him to go back to his apartment, study them up, and advance a cyber attack that was far more sophisticated than he'd ever been able to conduct before."

McClurg has also seen interlinked threats that run in the other direction, using cyber vulnerabilities to attack physical entities. "Supervisory control data acquisition systems (SCDAs) can be remotely accessed in order to control physical systems which, if not properly secured, can be compromised to undermine the physical well-being of the systems those SCDAs control," he said.

Well, you may think, certainly these types of threats exist, but if physical and information security are excellent, it shouldn't matter if they're separate technologically or organizationally. The lockpick wouldn't make it into the data room if physical security was done right, and the hacker cannot reach the SCDA if information security is doing its job. To that, McClurg replied with a name: "Harold James Nicholson. One of the highest-ranking spies ever arrested in the Central Intelligence Agency (CIA). There are few places that have cyber security or physical security as good as that agency's. There's always the possibility of a trusted insider looking for ways to slip through."

Interlinked threats are best addressed through an interlinked response. A unified model of management in which different units share information and alerts can help raise flags. Similarly, security systems that monitor and log both physical and cyber events, and may even respond to them in a coordinated fashion, provide a crucial extra layer of protection against interlinked threats.

COLLABORATIVE MODELS PROVIDE BUSINESS VALUE

Both a unified structure of security management and a judicious use of interoperable systems technology truly can provide significant business value.

The unified structure under which Honeywell Global Security operates allowed McClurg to find efficiencies in risk assessment, for one. "With our business hat on, we're looking for ways to deliver security services in the most economically efficient manner possible. An example in the business world would be combining IT and physical security risk assessments. Traditionally, you knock on the door of a business unit one week saying 'We need to do an IT security review'—you disrupt business, engage the employees in trying to extract the information necessary, and produce a report that you want them to read and digest. Then two weeks later, you knock on the door and the physical security guys do the same thing all over again. Convergence in that realm means doing your risk assessments in a converged way as well, so you knock only once, and you deliver one final product that provides full-spectrum visibility to your customers as to what the issues are and what action they should take. Less time, less money; more comprehensive, more enlightening. And you're more likely to be engaged and viewed as a true partner in the business environment rather than a cost of doing business."

On the technology side, Terry Neely of PlaSec Inc. described how interoperable access control systems can provide benefits. "Once you're able to authenticate a person's identity, you're able to correlate it to his physical location, and you can start writing all kinds of very nice authentication rules as to what he's allowed to do where and when. It can be anything from financial institution regulations and governance, to setting different access provisions if you're out of the country and you want to transmit intellectual property information from your hotel room, for example," said Neely. "One of the things I see happening is physical access control becoming accessible to IT tools and practices, so that if there's a change in the security posture on the network it can also put my doors into two-factor authentication or lock my data center doors."

Dave Kent has used interoperable systems to both centrally monitor global operations and to keep watch on his company's supply chain. "We have a centralized program for product security, and the tools that are at work in that system notify us when we have supply chain problems, even just operational supply chain problems, or products that haven't arrived on time or have been stolen. There's no better example of a business driver than being able to deliver product to your customers, and this investigative process, the security of the product, the network aspect or control system for monitoring the product in the supply chain, are all interlinked and come back into one central system."

"Our service center is another good example," continued Kent. "We have 14 manufacturing plants and more than 100 locations, and we have one point of control with one access card all around the world, with four staff members handling it. And they're not only doing physical security, they're monitoring travelers around the world; they monitor the wireless intrusion system for the wireless networks; they have all sorts of intelligence coming in. The world is really just a virtual campus based on technology. You get the efficiencies of thinking like you're one location."

WORDS MATTER

A 2007 study developed by Deloitte for the Alliance for Enterprise Security Risk Management concluded that convergence was developing at a slow pace, and that visionaries were leading the way. Clearly, many factors play into this delay. Dave Kent noted that it's one thing to implement a unified management structure when your model can grow along with a growing company, and it's quite another to go to the management of an 80-year-old organization and say, "I'm going to tear down what you've built and put in this because it's a better idea." This is the situation in which many leaders find themselves. PlaSec's Neely claimed that end users want what interoperable systems have to offer, but in many cases they don't have the desire, money, or expertise to do the programming required to make systems communicate. In this sense, closed, proprietary systems continue to take a toll on what can and can't be done.

So yes, it is simplistic to blame the slow growth of interoperability and structural unification on the word we use to describe them. Yes, other factors are at play. Yes, if you use the word carefully and specifically in your program, you and your colleagues can share a clear understanding of its meaning. But how we speak impacts how we think as well as how we're viewed by others. If "convergence" lacks meaning, both within our industry and in the eyes of the businesspeople you need to influence, maybe it's time to leave it behind.

CHAPTER 3

What Are the Characteristics of a Good Relationship Between Corporate Security and Information Security?

With insight from Lou Magnotti, chief information officer, U.S. House of Representatives; Liz Lancaster, director of member services, Security Executive Council; Lorna Koppel, vice president and chief information security officer, Iron Mountain; and John Masserini, information security officer, Dow Jones & Co.

In this chapter, four experienced security and information security professionals respond to the question, what are the characteristics of a good relationship between corporate security and information security?

LOU MAGNOTTI, CHIEF INFORMATION OFFICER, U.S. HOUSE OF REPRESENTATIVES

There is nothing more important than communication in any effective relationship; it is the foundation of competency. The communication between corporate security and information security must be open and candid, while maintaining a professional respect for each other's knowledge, areas of responsibility, and experience. Looking back at my 28-year career, the current emphasis on convergence of physical, industrial, operational, and information security seems almost like a step back in time. During the late 1970s and early 1980s, we were all one multi-disciplined security department. But the computer security folks, myself included, fought hard to be recognized as a separate security discipline. Moving forward, we can have the best of both worlds and really make a difference if we remain committed to communication, operate from understanding our business requirements, and develop risk mitigation strategies as a team. The relationship must typify the fighter pilots' slogan, "I've got your six [back]!"

LIZ LANCASTER, DIRECTOR OF MEMBER SERVICES, SECURITY EXECUTIVE COUNCIL

Over the last several years, there has been a push to collaborate among security groups to identify, manage, and mitigate risk as a collective effort. Rather than owning business risks, security leaders (and their groups) are evolving into subject matter experts who provide consultation related to risk mitigation to the rest of the organization. This push is shifting security responsibilities to individual stakeholders in an ongoing effort to make security part of everyone's corporate responsibility. A good relationship between corporate and information security involves listening to issues of peer groups, providing a sounding board, and meeting face-to-face. Awareness evolves from gaining an understanding of risks to each business unit in your respective areas. Innovate by sharing ideas and information. Define risk management roles together based on skill-sets. Demonstrate leadership in areas of expertise. Drive program success together, and measure and communicate that success to senior leadership.

LORNA KOPPEL, VICE PRESIDENT AND CHIEF INFORMATION SECURITY OFFICER (CISO), IRON MOUNTAIN

Working together successfully means you can pick up the phone at any time and discuss concerns, ideas, etc. and work on solutions without fear of turf politics getting in the way. Either area, corporate security or information security, should be able to lead initiatives and be trusted that they will look out for the interests important to the other team and know when to bring them in. Trust means leaders and staff at all levels feel comfortable communicating honestly and openly across organizational lines. Both areas must take a shared approach to protecting the company because, frankly, risk mitigation overlaps both areas. There should be respect for each other's unique skills and acknowledgment of inherent weaknesses. Information security can help corporate security work through IT processes. Corporate security has access to resources and specific training in areas with law enforcement, interrogations, investigations, and overall personnel security that information security folks don't typically have.

JOHN MASSERINI, INFORMATION SECURITY OFFICER, DOW JONES & CO.

A strong relationship between information security and corporate security is critical for the success of both and goes far beyond the asset management/loss prevention realm. Being a global organization, we rely on our corporate security counterparts to enforce policies on behalf of information security. With offices ranging from five to 2,000 people, reliable physical security of data center and office space access allows development of technology solutions with less restrictive risk profiles, thereby enabling our user population to drive business. Additionally, the Global Information Security Office owns business continuity, disaster recovery, and crisis management planning—all of which are dependent not only on corporate security but facilities management as well. Our success in planning is directly linked to the support and execution of the plans by corporate security groups around the world. A strong level of trust between the two organizations, and constant communication, enable both groups to complement each other to drive down risk.

PART *2*

Emerging Issues in
Information Protection

CHAPTER 4

Mobile Insecurity

By Derek Benz, chief information security officer for Honeywell International.

In a world where convenience is king, global markets demand mobility, and the sun never sets on business, the idea of increased security chafes like a leash on 21st-century businesspeople. It seems every time we turn on the television, there's another hacker incident, another nation-state poised to pounce on our indiscretions, another tale of the rising shadow of organized cybercrime—but many people figure that, statistically speaking, they'll be able to dodge the bullet. It won't happen to them. And certainly not to something they carry with them, right by their side, wherever they go.

Enter the world of mobile insecurity. This is where our employees spend their waking lives: the airports, train stations, subways, coffee shops, and even the Olympic five-star hotel in Beijing. They travel everywhere, they eat wherever convenient, they chat on their phones while hailing a cab. They are the nonstop machine driving value to your bottom line. But forget about hackers for a minute. The real risk may be in simply being human. And humans have a habit of leaving their stuff just lying around.

Loss of mobile assets is on the rise. According to Pointsec Mobile Technologies, a 2005 survey of a major Chicago-area taxicab company revealed the staggering loss of 85,000 cell phones, 21,000 PDAs, and over 4,000 laptops left behind in a six-month time period. In their words:

> *Pointsec first commissioned the study four years ago in London; this year's results indicated a significant worsening in the problem, with 71 percent more laptops and 350 percent more pocket PCs/PDAs being left behind in that city than in 2001.*[1]

---

[1]"Taxis Hailed as Black Hole for Lost Cell Phones and PDAs, as Confidential Data Gets Taken for a Ride," Check Point Software Technologies Ltd. press release, January 24, 2005, https://www.checkpoint.com/press/pointsec/2005/01-24a.html, accessed April 29, 2014.

Those statistics are nearly a decade old. Things have been spiraling since. In 2012, for example, a report from Lookout Labs found that Americans lose, on average, one mobile phone per year, for a total of $30 billion in lost mobile phones in 2011.[2]

In 2008, Dell released the results of a study conducted by the Ponemon Institute that found that more than 12,000 laptops are lost by businesspeople in U.S. airports every week.[3] Not every month or every year—every week. These aren't thefts. Like the taxicab reference above, these are what people leave behind, like cuff links or earrings, and many of these forgotten items store data that could lead to lawsuits, stock dives, and identity theft.

We've got to make a change in how we safeguard our mobile assets, and there's a lot of technology on the horizon aimed to help us do just that. In the meantime, here are a few suggestions you could implement within your organization now.

- Leave the laptops behind. Laptops are our biggest issue: they have more data capacity than most mobile assets, and they're where we do our work. One change you can make right now is to set up a policy that allows travel with laptops only on an exception basis, allowing your travelers to bring only their BlackBerry or iPhone (or whatever multi-function PDA you like). These devices can be encrypted and can also be remotely wiped when reported stolen. You can also get them replaced in no time. If you meet resistance to the policy, consider that airlines are beginning to charge for luggage and are severely limiting how much you can bring on board. After your travelers pick up the wreckage of their laptop from checked baggage, they'll start to support your policy with more enthusiasm. And on a brighter note, more and more executives I talk to are starting to travel light. While this might be more out of convenience than security awareness, it amounts to the same thing: reduced risk.
- Use a loaner pool. The most common reason I hear for why a traveler simply must carry a laptop on board is that the airplane acts as a second office. This is where they catch up on all their

---

[2]Roger Yu, "Lost Cellphones Added up Fast in 2011," *USA Today*, March 23, 2012, http://usatoday30.usatoday.com/tech/news/story/2012-03-22/lost-phones/53707448/1.
[3]"New Study Reveals up to 12,000 Laptop Computers Lost Weekly and up to 600,000 Lost Annually in U.S. Airports," Ponemon Institute, accessed March 24, 2014, http://www.ponemon.org/news-2/8.

e-mails and put the finishing touches on their slide decks. It's a good point. The solution for employees in this situation is to set up a loaner pool in your organization. Chances are, travelers have to set up their travel in advance, using a travel agency or approved booking process. Make the loaner laptop part of the process—but make it an exception, not the rule. Also, ensure that any loaner is freshly imaged/wiped, with only standard applications. Think about including an encryption program to allow travelers to secure those files that they bring with them.

- Institute a loss reporting policy. Missing laptops and cell phones are a big deal. As such, employees tend to report their loss, which can lead to the recovery of the asset or allow time to mitigate the risk. However, employees rarely report losing smaller mobile devices, such as USB flash drives or burned CDs. If these inexpensive and small items are lost, employees simply get a replacement. Considering how much confidential data can be squeezed onto one of these devices, this seems imprudent. Institute a travel policy that requires the reporting of any lost or stolen mobile assets, no matter how small. Better safe than sorry.
- Secure all mobile devices. Whatever device the traveler takes with him or her, you'll want it secured. For laptops, consider whole disk encryption solutions, such as McAfee's SafeBoot. For cell phones, ensure your devices are encrypted and capable of remote wipe. For thumb drives and other data storage devices, start thinking about encryption solutions. This way, if the asset is lost, your company's reputation isn't.

In the near future, all our mobile assets will continue to converge into one single device, probably not unlike an enterprise-strength iPhone. These devices be fully encrypted and remotely wipable, have GPS tracking, and be replaceable at little cost. Human nature won't change anytime soon. We'll continue to leave stuff in taxis and hotel rooms. But technology and simple processes should go a long way to help ensure that the loss won't end up on Wall Street.

CHAPTER 5

Security in Cloud Computing:
How Is It Different?

With insight from Mark Estberg, senior director of risk and compliance manage-ment, online services security and compliance, Microsoft; Jim Reavis, co-founder and executive director, Cloud Security Alliance; Greg Kane, director, IT and prod-uct technology, Security Executive Council; and Jeff M. Spivey, director, Security Risk Management Inc.

In this chapter, four experienced security and information security pro-fessionals respond to the question, from a risk management perspec-tive, how is security in cloud computing different from security in outsourced services?

MARK ESTBERG, SENIOR DIRECTOR OF RISK AND COMPLIANCE MANAGEMENT, ONLINE SERVICES SECURITY AND COMPLIANCE, MICROSOFT

There are more similarities than differences from a risk management perspective. The fundamental problem remains the same, which is whether transferring risk outside of your organization is the right choice. What is different is that there are fewer accepted standards to establish a trusted transfer of risk. Outsourcing has matured to a level where contractual terms and conditions are relatively routine and mechanisms exist to verify security claims of an outsource provider. Cloud computing lacks these practices for efficient supplier and cus-tomer understanding. Certifications based on industry best practices such as IS0 27001 and methods to verify whether specific security capabilities are in place and operating such as SAS 70 types I and II are a start. The same types of capabilities to allow for a trusted trans-fer of risk for outsourced services need to be developed for the cloud computing environment.

JIM REAVIS, CO-FOUNDER AND EXECUTIVE DIRECTOR, CLOUD SECURITY ALLIANCE

While there are many similarities, the differences are profound. The economic optimization of computing as a utility puts pressure on some traditional data center practices that seek to mitigate risks. The location of an enterprise's assets may be unknowable; commingling of your data with other enterprises may be common; and isolating and extracting your data may be more difficult. In general, the physical segregation of computer systems and dedicated outsourced employees managing/ manipulating those systems is missing, and all security controls must be logical, which may not be well understood by the customer.

GREG KANE, DIRECTOR, IT AND PRODUCT TECHNOLOGY, SECURITY EXECUTIVE COUNCIL

I would posit that security in cloud computing is actually not significantly different than security in outsourced services. You are essentially expanding the scope of your organization to include a third party. If you have a robust and reliable process to assess and maintain the security of outsourcing at your organization, then you probably have a good start on securing your cloud computing initiatives. Whether the decision is to use outsourcing or cloud computing, your organization cannot relax its risk mitigation posture. If you are not assured that your providers are maintaining the security and privacy of your information, then you can't afford to use them. Outsourcing is relatively more mature and as such its providers tend to readily acknowledge the specific security requirements of their customers. Organizations must work to get these same assurances from their cloud computing providers. Security practitioners need to make senior management aware of the risks of moving to cloud computing, just as they did for outsourcing initiatives. Get ahead of the business on this. Having policies in place encourages your organization to include them as requirements when seeking a provider of cloud computing services.

JEFF M. SPIVEY, DIRECTOR, SECURITY RISK MANAGEMENT INC.

Risk management uses a framework to evaluate risks of emerging technologies: identifying risks and then managing them in support of the enterprise goals. Understand that a cloud can be private or public. The risks that virtualization technology exercises in a cloud are a concern of bits/bytes, but when a cloud is public, there are both technical risks and all the risks of outsourcing added to the mix. Governance, risk compliance, control framework moving across virtual layers while provisioning resources—these are complicated and require technical frameworks, third-party validation, and transparency of operations for public cloud providers. Outsourcing requires precise service-level agreements covering important process- and security-related responsibilities. The customer company should maintain any organizational core competencies in the course of outsourcing and thoroughly understand virtualization/emerging cloud risks so that the organization's interests are being managed and are not dependent on the cloud provider.

CHAPTER 6

The Security Risks of Web-Based Applications in the Workplace

With lessons learned from Chris Berg, senior director, corporate security and safety, Symantec Corporation; Leslie K. Lambert, vice president, chief information officer, Sun Microsystems; and Kathleen Kotwica, executive vice president and chief knowledge strategist, Security Executive Council.

In this chapter, three experienced security and information security professionals respond to the questions, should I allow web-based applications to be accessed from company computers? If I do, how do I avoid the inherent security risks?

CHRIS BERG, SENIOR DIRECTOR, CORPORATE SECURITY AND SAFETY, SYMANTEC CORPORATION

Employees' use of web-based technologies, such as YouTube, Facebook, or Twitter, while at work is a growing risk for many corporations. Companies see a full spectrum of issues including the predictable productivity losses, the introduction of viruses, and exposure to malicious software attacks. Additionally, there's reputational risk relating to privacy concerns, and the evolving risk that's illustrated when employees' comments and opinions are posted to sites using company-owned infrastructure. To prevent such problems, many companies start by rolling out a written policy, a clear statement about the organization's perspective and management's commitment to appropriately dealing with the risk. Some restrict access to web-based technologies and others are rethinking risk assessment methodologies and solutions to adapt.

LESLIE K. LAMBERT, VICE PRESIDENT, CHIEF INFORMATION OFFICER, SUN MICROSYSTEMS

Methods of communicating and collaborating by enterprise users are emerging faster than we can keep up with them. The easy answer is to shut them down, but that's not reality. Employees are jumping on these technologies and using them to get their work done. We decided to deal with new technologies within the framework of information security policies already in place. Risk to your company depends on what tools are used and what company information is entered or transacted within those tools. Internal tools are likely more secure; external tools and the data stored on their systems may not follow existing company policies on how to handle company information.

KATHLEEN KOTWICA, EXECUTIVE VICE PRESIDENT AND CHIEF KNOWLEDGE STRATEGIST, SECURITY EXECUTIVE COUNCIL

For some companies it makes sense to use web-based technologies. It depends on what the company does. A media or consumer goods company may use social networking apps to enhance its marketing reach. A start-up may use collaborative applications (e.g., instant messaging internally) to speed up research and development (R&D). For a defense contractor this may be too high a risk and there should be zero tolerance. Typical policies of Internet use may already cover appropriate personal use or business use. However, if a guideline or policy was written more than five years ago, it may need updating. There is a big difference risk-wise between an employee surfing to an inappropriate content site and an employee accidentally divulging company intellectual property on a social networking site; the former is a nuisance, while the latter can bring a company down.

CHAPTER 7

Leveraging Information Lifecycle Management for Convergence and Compliance

By Miki Calero, CISM, PMP, CSO for the City of Columbus, Ohio.

Protecting the confidentiality, integrity, and availability of information assets should be a convergence endeavor. The Information Lifecycle Management (ILM) strategy assures protection and enables compliance with both information and physical requirements of existing laws, rules, and regulations.

The Storage Network Industry Association (SNIA) defines ILM as the policies, processes, practices, services, and tools used to align the business value of information with the most appropriate and cost-effective infrastructure from the time information is created through its final disposition. While ILM has its roots in the storage industry, approaching compliance from an ILM perspective enables the convergence of areas such as information classification policy with incident response processes, or physical access control services with audit log management tools.

Information has always followed a lifecycle; organizations have always used document management, content management, and records management methods, all of which are functions inherent to ILM. Documents have business value, physical records must be warehoused, and content is retained or disposed of. SNIA makes sure security convergence is inherent to ILM through the work of publications such as its *Storage Security Best Practices.*[1]

SNIA's Security Technical Work Group (TWG) says that storage security represents the "convergence of the storage, networking, and security disciplines, technologies, and methodologies for the purpose of protecting and securing digital assets."[2] It presents the best practices as

[1]Eric Hibbard, "SNIA Storage Security Best Practices," Storage Networking Industry Association (SNIA), 2009, page 6, http://www.snia.org/sites/default/education/tutorials/2009/spring/security/EricHibbard_SNIA_Storage_Security-BestPractices.pdf.
[2]Ibid.

the means to a holistic approach for organizations to secure their storage systems/ecosystems. SNIA also sponsors security forums such as the Storage Security Industry Forum (SSIF) that promote collaboration between members, volunteers, and other groups. The resources they produce, such as the *SSIF Risk Assessment Toolkit* and the *Cryptographic Use Cases and the Rationale for End-to-End Security* tutorial, provide the perspective for organizations to have converged security and achieve compliance.

SNIA counts on its 10 years in existence and a membership that includes major vendors to bolster its credibility and promote the adoption of its standards. Nonetheless, the association's standing has been recently counterbalanced by criticism of its leadership and membership structure, which skews voting power toward larger vendors—those with the largest membership fees.

Coincidentally, it is these larger members that, in an effort to distinguish their offerings from the competition and increase market share, introduce non-standard terminology (e.g., Intelligent Information Management [IIM]). Beyond SNIA, vendor definitions, processes, practices, and services have become even more divergent: ILM is now synonymous with DLM (D referring to data). In acknowledgment to the importance (or marketability) of security, data becomes protected, yielding PDLM.

Issues such as these increase the challenges security groups face in pursuing an ILM-based security strategy; nonetheless, the case for ILM as a catalyst for convergence and compliance is strong—and is stronger when considering the *quantitative* risk of non-compliance with laws, regulations, and rules, and the significant investment of resources necessary to implement the supporting organizational change.

Even partial adoption of unified security policies, processes, practices, and services will yield improvement. Leveraging ILM for security convergence will yield the true benefit: protection of information assets. With security in place, compliance will follow.

CHAPTER 8

Preventing Identity Theft by Protecting Your Data

With insight from Tony Heredia, director of investigations and assets protection for Target Corporation.

A man walking down an empty residential street opens a mailbox and shoves its contents—including a credit card statement containing four convenience checks—into his jacket. A hacker breaks into a corporate database and downloads information on all the company's 1,200 employees. A group collects social security numbers from a phishing scam that asks e-mail recipients to update their personal information on a sham website. Teenagers watch a retail employee throwing paper transaction logs into a trash bin behind a shopping center and dig them out once she's gone. An organized gang pays a hospital worker to hand over the medical or insurance information of patients in bulk.

The problem with identity theft is that it's all of these things, and its results include all types of fraud, from credit card and check fraud to medical and government benefits fraud, as well as blackmail. Because identity theft is such a broad and perhaps ill-defined crime category, it's often shrouded in misconceptions, and its potential as a damaging threat is often underestimated.

In most of the above scenarios, the consumer is the immediate intended victim who stands to lose from the information theft. Businesses and organizations—the corporation whose database is breached, the company whose logo is on the phishing e-mail, the retailer whose dumpster is searched, the hospital and the insurance companies that lose patient information—also stand to suffer significant long-term consequences.

A RAMPANT PROBLEM

There's no way to accurately estimate the number of identity thefts that occur annually. Many companies and organizations track reported cases of various types of identity theft, but few can monitor every method, and since the crime may go undiscovered or unreported for a long time, it is possible existing estimates are the tip of the iceberg. Several estimates place the number of incidents between 8 and 10 million each year. The Identity Theft Resource Center, which continually catalogs confirmed electronic and paper data breaches, reports 260 breaches in 2014 as of April 29, with more than 8 million individual records exposed.[1] More than a quarter of those records are accounted for by a possible data security attack reported by Michaels Stores in January.

It is this type of breach that sends shivers up the spines of retailers, banks, and other companies that handle financial data. Whereas other types of identity theft, like the recovery of paper records outside a store, generally impact a limited number of customers and may easily avoid attention, the high-level financial data security breach quickly exposes millions of records, making for spectacular headline news.

POTENTIAL COSTS IN THE BILLIONS

In 2007, Forrester Research released a study called "Calculating the Cost of a Security Breach" that estimated the business costs of a data breach at anywhere from $90 to $305 per customer record, depending on the type of company and the profile of the breach.[2] The number has almost certainly grown in the years since, given inflation and the growing complexity and scale of attacks. When millions of accounts are exposed, the final figure is staggering.

Impacted businesses must front the cost of notifying customers of the breach, satisfying applicable fines, paying legal fees, instituting new protections, and investigating complaints. And in theft of credit card data specifically, victimized consumers are generally not held responsible for fraudulent charges, so banks or businesses end up bearing the direct financial losses.

Reputational loss and the loss of future sales take a toll as well. According to a recent Pew Research Internet Project survey, "growing numbers of internet users (50%) say they are worried about the amount of

[1]"ITRC 2014 Breach List," Identity Theft Resource Center (IRTC), April 29, 2014, http://www.idtheftcenter.org/images/breach/ITRC_Breach_Report_2014.pdf.
[2]Khalid Klark, et al, "Calculating the Cost of a Security Breach," Forrester Research, April 10, 2007, http://www.forrester.com/Calculating+The+Cost+Of+A+Security+Breach/fulltext/-/E-RES42082.

personal information about them that is online—a figure that has jumped from 33% who expressed such worry in 2009."[3] When coupled with a publicized security breach, these persistent worries could lead Internet users to avoid shopping online at a certain retailer. Also, when the data exposed in a breach is financial, it seems to elicit a stronger response from consumers than, say, the loss of social security numbers or birth dates, because the danger feels more immediate and hits them where it hurts: in their bank accounts.

THE FINGER POINTS AT SECURITY

Any damage to the company as a whole is damaging to security, because the bottom line impacts every business unit. But in the case of a network breach, security is directly in the line of fire. When senior management and the board come to find out how this could have happened, they'll head straight for security's door. Fortunately, it seems that security is not always the sacrificial lamb anymore. Security executives at companies that have suffered some of the biggest breaches in recent years still have their jobs. But if major breaches occur, the public may call for the ousting of security leaders, their reputation will suffer inside and outside of the company, and they likely won't escape public embarrassment, since news outlets will be scouring their records and actions to find the hole that allowed the compromise.

PROTECTING FROM THE INSIDE

There are a number of things companies can do to protect themselves. The right defenses depend upon the type of company, its level of sophistication or experience in information protection, and how it stores and transmits different types of information. But all organizations should begin the hardening process with a comprehensive risk assessment that is regularly re-evaluated. If your organization doesn't have the expertise to do this in-house, hire a consultant to help you through the process. The risk assessment is the only way to identify the appropriate measures to shore up the holes in your organization's security program.

The risk assessment is also a requirement of nearly every law, guideline, and regulation governing the protection of sensitive information.

[3]Lee Rainie, et al, "Anonymity, Privacy, and Security Online," Pew Research Internet Project, September 5, 2013, http://www.pewinternet.org/2013/09/05/anonymity-privacy-and-security-online/.

Most industries and sectors are now subject to their own information protection requirements, with heavy fines and penalties for noncompliance. (For a partial list of security-related guidelines and regulations, visit https://www.securityexecutivecouncil.com/public/lrvc.)

These guidelines and requirements should be viewed as a help to the security program, not a hindrance. They provide guidance on how to prevent common attacks in various industries, taking some of the guesswork out of the risk mitigation process. However, compliance with the applicable laws and standards still does not guarantee protection against data breach. "Compliance is helpful, but compliance does not equal security," says Tony Heredia, director of investigations and assets protection for Target Corporation. According to Heredia, private industry must partner with the public sector to investigate and prevent data breaches if they hope to protect themselves from this threat.

PREVENTING THROUGH PARTNERSHIP

"There are two key reasons this problem needs to be addressed jointly," says Heredia. "First, the criminals who set out to breach networks are intent on beating any technological advances that are in place. They're spending all their time—24 hours a day—figuring that out. So you can't prevent everything with technology.

"Second, when something does happen, businesses need to partner with law enforcement to investigate it and rely on the criminal justice system to bring these people to justice. Both those groups need to understand the threat from a private-sector perspective, and they need the cooperation and help of the business' investigative resources."

Target believes this strongly enough to put their money where their mouth is. The company has been funding analysts at the National Cyber-Forensics and Training Alliance (NCFTA), which brings together subject matter experts from industry, academia, and government to provide advanced training and forensic analysis to reduce cyber vulnerability. Target has also positioned a full-time investigator at the Federal Bureau of Investigation's (FBI) Internet Crime Complaint Center for the last few years.

Public-private partnerships are useful for prevention as well as for investigation and prosecution. Says Heredia, "The Secret Service works with the Carnegie Mellon CERT Institute every year to do a survey of the private sector to better understand the trends around network breaches, network intrusions and personal information theft, and the more aware law enforcement is of what's going on in those enterprises, the better equipped they will be to handle those kinds of investigations." Shared information about how a company's networks are constructed, the kinds of things being seen in their intrusion detection system, and what the virus software is picking up can help crime labs and groups like the NCFTA develop better parameters to detect this activity before it causes damage and makes headlines.

CHAPTER 9

Protecting Your Organization's Intellectual Property

With insights from Mark A. Levett, unit chief, Counterintelligence Division, Federal Bureau of Investigation (FBI) Headquarters; Vincent Volpi, chairman and chief executive officer (CEO), PICA Corporation; Chris Cox, president, the Operations Security Professional's Association; and Marcy M. Forman, director, National Intellectual Property Rights Coordination Center.

In this chapter, four experienced security professionals respond to the question, how can I best protect my organization's intellectual property?

MARK A. LEVETT, UNIT CHIEF, COUNTERINTELLIGENCE DIVISION, FEDERAL BUREAU OF INVESTIGATION HEADQUARTERS

Foreign espionage accounts for annual losses in the United States exceeding $250 billion. The first step in protecting intellectual property (IP) is to clearly identify what unique company assets are considered critical to your business continuity. Precise identification of IP is critical when allocating scarce security resources to a counterintelligence (CI) protection plan.

The next step in risk management is to determine the threat to your IP. The FBI can assist in identifying the foreign espionage threat and the specific tradecraft utilized to steal IP. Tradecraft includes the recruitment of a trusted insider, cyber intrusions, and covert measures cloaked as overt business transactions. The FBI's Counterintelligence Division has a headquarters section and 56 field offices with Strategic Partnership Coordinators (SPCs) dedicated to assisting the private sector in identifying the threat to IP posed by foreign espionage. SPCs are able to provide CI Awareness briefings and CI Vulnerability Assessments to ensure companies have strong CI programs.

VINCENT VOLPI, CHAIRMAN AND CHIEF EXECUTIVE OFFICER, PICA CORPORATION

The first level of protection of intellectual property has to do with the creator. If the creator isn't under a solid contract and doesn't understand the importance of confidentiality and basic security precautions, all can be lost. Most creators are inventors, scientists, or artists, not lawyers or security professionals.

Maintaining "four-wall" security and information security (including "need-to-know" criteria) are other common basics. Otherwise, to commercialize IP requires that you share it with others. This includes people involved in legal, sourcing, marketing, and sales. Legal should be at the forefront, controlling everyone's use of IP by contracts that are strong, venue-specific, and enforceable. Contracts also need to contain audit, compliance, and penalty provisions.

Finally, you need a brand protection program designed around your budget and primary consuming and producing markets. You can't protect the world, so you have to protect the most important parts of it.

CHRIS COX, PRESIDENT, THE OPERATIONS SECURITY PROFESSIONAL'S ASSOCIATION

There are many things to consider when protecting your intellectual property. Of course, you'll need to copyright your work, when applicable, and physically protect your facilities using safes, surveillance, and whatever else would be cost efficient and effective. However, it's the human element that's all too often overlooked.

There's a saying within the operations security community: "If you don't know what you're trying to protect, how will you protect it?" In other words, if your employees don't know what information is critical to your organization, they can't be expected to know what they should protect, or how to do so.

Also, employees need to be trained to recognize and react to social engineering attempts, which are low-tech attempts to steal information by exploiting human nature. Once they can identify the critical information and understand the threats, all employees become part of your security team.

MARCY M. FORMAN, DIRECTOR, NATIONAL INTELLECTUAL PROPERTY RIGHTS COORDINATION CENTER

Take part in the fight to protect your rights. The National Intellectual Property Rights Coordination Center (IPR Center), hosted by U.S. Immigration and Customs Enforcement, is the government's leader for information related to potential criminal IPR violations. The IPR Center employs a true task-force model to optimize the roles and enforcement efforts of member agencies, while enhancing government-industry partnerships to support ongoing IPR enforcement initiatives. The center employs a three-pronged strategy, involving investigation to track down counterfeit goods, interdiction to stop them, and training and outreach to industry stakeholders and the public. Leads received from industry are analyzed and vetted by agency partners, and reviewed for criminal investigation or interdiction activity, as appropriate.

Start by visiting our website at www.ice.gov/pi/iprctr. There you will find contact information, links for reporting an alleged IPR violation and to the IPR Center Report, a newsletter with information on enforcement activities, and industry trends.

PART 3

Information Protection Regulations and Standards

CHAPTER 10

The PCI Data Security Standard: Compliance Lessons Learned

By Kenneth L. Davis, chief information security officer for Sun Health.

I have had the opportunity to talk to many chief security officers (CSO) and chief information security officers (CISO) about their experiences implementing and maintaining compliance with the Payment Card Industry (PCI) Data Security Standard (DSS). The PCI DSS is a well-thought-out contractual mandate, the result of a rare collaboration among commercial industries. It has been highly successful in demanding compliance from users of card services and levying stiff penalties for noncompliance.

In spite of this real incentive to comply, some executives continue to struggle with implementing the security standard for a variety of reasons.

SOMETIMES EXECUTIVES MISUNDERSTAND THE NATURE OF COMPLIANCE

After talking to several CSOs and CISOs struggling with the DSS, I've noticed that many business leaders think of PCI compliance and assurance as a one-time, gap-mitigation event that only applies to technology and is conducted six weeks prior to the arrival of the PCI auditors.

To counter such misunderstandings, the CSO and CISO must combine organizational forces and create partnerships and awareness sessions with each other and then with the business. This will help them find champions who will support a more holistic approach to compliance and assurance. If business executives are only asking about PCI once a year, it is time to get out of the office and shake some trees to get the discussions going. There is no advantage in waiting, and rarely is six weeks enough time to do anything that requires the involvement of more than one organization.

PCI DSS IS SEEN AND MANAGED SOLELY AS AN INFORMATION TECHNOLOGY PROJECT

Nothing builds organizational and leadership distrust, back-biting, and "real estate" wars more than leaving key organizational stakeholders out of the creation and implementation of strategic and tactical plans. Having worked in IT for practically all of my professional life, I understand that IT experts often feel a great deal of personal ownership over some projects, and they sometimes espouse an attitude that life begins and ends in IT. However, I also know that many business organizations and stakeholders, fed up with such attitudes, staunchly resist any new ideas, partnerships, and requests originating out of IT. Over the years we may have come to earn such snubbing. Regardless, such an environment does not promote business success.

To counter these cultural problems, many IT organizations now present IT as a service to the business. Reaching out to strategic partners, involving key individuals, and seeking to understand and to be understood—these actions help businesses reach compliance and build successful assurance programs.

BUSINESS UNITS DISAGREE ON THE RIGHT APPROACH TO ACHIEVING COMPLIANCE

The PCI DSS communicates people, process, and technology requirements for compliance. But it doesn't communicate exactly how it should be implemented or what product must be used. In the IT world, product selection often becomes a point of debate and contention. IT people sometimes act as if a certain vendor's hardware appliance or software product is an extension of their personal identity. If you run into the chief information officer (CIO), get your benchmarking supporting material ready, because if you decide on a product other than his or her personal favorite, this individual will debate and test your patience until you decide you a) have wasted too much time on this decision and give in, or b) would rather be selling ceramic horses at flea markets.

If your boss or board of directors continues to ask questions about your implementation of PCI DSS after you have already presented your approach to compliance, it may mean you have not established enough credibility to satisfy other voiced concerns. Take time to shop your strategy and tactical plans. Be sure to involve not only the people who agree with your opinion, but those who may not as well.

You are one of many on the same journey to compliance. Take advantage of all of the available resources to assist you in making the right decisions. But above all, understand what the business expectations are for compliance and continue to stay in touch with these expectations, because they often will change two or three times before you have succeeded in implementing the "right" compliance and assurance program.

CHAPTER 11

Is Your Data Leaking?

By Bob Pappagianopoulos, corporate director of technical services and operations and CISO at Partners Healthcare System in Boston, Massachusetts.

Many surveys have suggested that the number of known records containing confidential personal information involved in security breaches measures in the hundreds of millions. In today's regulatory environment, the compromise of such confidential data costs more than consumer confidence and the price of resolution—it costs hard cash in the form of heavy fines. A number of high-profile laws and regulations require that companies take steps to protect personal data or face the consequences.

But how and where do we protect that data, and how do we do it without adversely affecting the business?

Data at rest (on your disk drives) needs to be secured. We all make sure that the data centers are secure, access to the data is controlled, and tight physical controls are checked and rechecked, but we also need to ensure that data is not leaving the organization in an unauthorized way or, when authorized, in an insecure way. When it does, it is known as *data leakage.*

Our task is to minimize this risk, but how?

Here are some steps that you can do to help mitigate your risks:

1. Create a chart of "risk vectors." This is a list of all the ways data can leave your organization.
   a. First, quantify each risk as high, medium, or low. You can do this by creating a 1–100 scale, with 100 being "high risk" based on risk, probability, and impact. NIST 800-30, Risk Management Guide for Information Technology Systems, Section 3.7.1, does a great job of explaining how to quantify risks.
   b. On a piece of paper or on your computer, draw a circle and put your company name in the middle. This represents your data. Draw lines coming out of your circle. At the end of each line,

draw another, smaller circle, and in each circle, label the various ways data can leave your organization. These may include hackers, removable media, FTP, laptops, etc. Color these as follows:

RED = Unauthorized. These need to stop.

BLUE = Authorized. These need to be secured.

The larger the circle, the bigger the risk factor.

2. Prioritize each vector based on:
   a. Cost of the solution;
   b. Amount of reduction of risk; and
   c. Hours of resources needed.

   You may find you have some "low-hanging fruit" and some costly but large-gain projects.

3. Create separate project teams to work on each risk vector, making sure they communicate often to maintain synergy between the teams.

4. Recalibrate every three months to take into account changing risks and priorities.

No one can ever stop all risks. If you try to, you may cripple your business. It is important to determine your target and create a metric to track your progress towards that goal. A risk vector chart can be an excellent tool to use not only for compliance and auditing, but also for project overview and budgeting. Such a metric will help you communicate your team's progress every step of the way.

CHAPTER 12

Aiming for National Cybersecurity

With insight from Lynn Mattice, former CSO of Boston Scientific; Theresa Payton, former White House CIO under President George W. Bush and a Security Executive Council Emeritus Faculty Content Expert; Tom Patterson, a business advisor on security, commerce, and governance and author of the book Mapping Security: The Corporate Security Sourcebook for Today's Global Economy; *Hord Tipton, former CIO of the U.S. Department of the Interior and current executive director of (ISC)²; Louis Magnotti, CIO for the U.S. House of Representatives; and William Crowell, former deputy director of the National Security Agency, current chairman of the Senior Advisory Board to the Director of National Intelligence, and a member of the Security Executive Council's Board of Advisors.*

Security has had more than 20 years to adjust to life in the Information Age. That's the equivalent of two or three lifetimes in high-tech years. But it seems every time we feel closest to truly securing our networks, data, and information, cybersecurity once again slithers out of our reach. Why is that?

In part, it's because quickly evolving technology turns threats and mitigation techniques into living, breathing things. It's also because cybersecurity isn't just about *each* of us; it's about *all* of us. Individual users, businesses, and agencies across the globe have excelled at protecting their cyber assets. But individual efforts, while critical, aren't enough. Information technology connects us all, sometimes more closely than we would prefer. We all share the risks and the responsibility.

CROSS-SECTOR FAILURES

Back in 2009, a *Wall Street Journal* report claimed foreign "cyberspies" had penetrated the U.S. power grid and left behind malicious software.[1] This is a prime example of the interconnectedness of our cyber existence. If our power grid were to be compromised and

---

[1]Siobhan Gorman, "Electricity Grid in U.S. Penetrated by Spies," *Wall Street Journal*, April 8, 2009, http://online.wsj.com/news/articles/SB123914805204099085.

manipulated for malicious purposes, it would pose significant problems for the electric industry in the form of damage, fines, loss of revenue, and more. It would cause problems for other privately owned businesses, which could lose significant revenue during prolonged or targeted power outages, and which could stand at greater risk of theft and looting in such circumstances. It would also create issues for the public sector, which would have to expend extra resources to confront a potential increase in crime and unrest that extended outages might bring, and which could lose some of its capability to effectively deploy defenses in the event of a simultaneous terrorist attack, for instance.

In the years since the *Wall Street Journal* story broke, we have only seen more and more significant critical infrastructure security breaches. In February 2014, a report was prepared by the Minority Staff of the Homeland Security and Governmental Affairs Committee to summarize the federal government's track record on cybersecurity and critical infrastructure. As Republican Senator Tom Coburn (OK) explained:

> *Data on the nation's weakest dams, including those which could kill Americans if they failed, were stolen by a malicious intruder. Nuclear plants' confidential cybersecurity plans have been left unprotected. Blueprints for the technology undergirding the New York Stock Exchange were exposed to hackers. Examples like [these] underscore for many the importance of increased federal involvement in protecting the nation's privately owned critical infrastructure.*[2]

For private businesses outside of critical infrastructure, their place in the chain of cybersecurity is particularly important. A data breach can have a major impact on a company's bottom line. For example, consider the Target security breach that came to light in late 2013. What would become known as the biggest retail hack in U.S. history cost Target $61 million through February 1, 2014, and that price tag is likely to increase.[3] But businesses' well-being also strongly impacts the state of the nation. Coordinated, malicious attacks on private businesses could degrade an already struggling economy, and economic

[2]The Minority Staff of the Homeland Security and Governmental Affairs Committee, "The Federal Government's Track Record on Cybersecurity and Critical Infrastructure," February 4, 2014, http://www.coburn.senate.gov/public/index.cfm?a=Files.Serve&File_id=f1d97a51-aca9-499f-a516-28eb872748c0.

[3]Michael Riley, et al, "Missed Alarms and 40 Million Stolen Credit Card Numbers: How Target Blew It," *Bloomberg Businessweek*, March 13, 2014, http://www.businessweek.com/articles/2014-03-13/target-missed-alarms-in-epic-hack-of-credit-card-data.

instability is historically associated with political turmoil, unrest, and increased crime.

Loss of trade secrets to foreign entities—as well as loss of information on sensitive projects by private government contractors—could bolster the economic and military strength of other countries at the same time. According to Lynn Mattice, former CSO of Boston Scientific and chair of the Board of Advisors of the Security Executive Council, "A recent report to Congress from the National Counterintelligence Executive highlighted that over 108 countries, both friend and foe, are actively stealing intellectual property from U.S. businesses to help bolster the competitive posture of their own economies."

The public sector and the private sector—both critical infrastructure and other business—are inextricably linked; a cybersecurity failure on the part of one could mean a new threat for all.

WHY ALL THE ATTENTION NOW?

Of course, the federal government, critical infrastructure, and other private companies have all been working for years to shore up cybersecurity gaps, some more wholeheartedly than others. Why is the spotlight suddenly shining so brightly on this issue?

One reason is the election of President Barack Obama, who promised to give it a hard look. "You have an administration that's increased the focus on leveraging social collaboration technologies, and the focus on furthering the agenda of the nation and leveraging technology," says Theresa Payton, former White House CIO under President George W. Bush and a Security Executive Council Emeritus Faculty Content Expert. "With that change in administration, the media have really started to look at and have an enhanced understanding of what's going on with cyber globally and in the United States. So in a sense, it's all about timing."

Another reason is the documented increase in the sophistication and number of cyberattacks. Experts agree that the types of threats we're facing now are dramatically different than they were even 12 months ago. "The nature of the threat has changed from casual attacks to very well-financed, substantial, well-delivered attacks," says Tom Patterson, a business advisor on security, commerce, and governance and author of the book *Mapping Security: The Corporate Security Sourcebook for Today's Global Economy.* "These advanced threats require equally advanced countermeasures for everybody now."

Hord Tipton, former CIO of the U.S. Department of the Interior and current executive director of (ISC)^2, explained, "We've always played this game with the hacking and attacking community, trying to catch up and get on an even par with them. But the evidence and data collected seems to indicate we're falling behind."

These increases can be chalked up in part to the slump in the world economy, according to Payton. "In desperate times, you see a run-up on traditional crimes, and now that cybercrime is becoming more mainstream, it's following the same pattern. I think this does put us more at risk; obviously the more somebody tries to get into your fortress, the more potential they have to find the weak link in the chain, so to speak. But at the same time, from a leadership perspective, the media attention on this topic is creating the positive impact of a heightened awareness of the threats."

SHARING IS KEY TO SUCCESS

Louis Magnotti, CIO for the U.S. House of Representatives, is one of many who believe cybersecurity isn't complete without coordinated protection across sectors. "An IP address doesn't care if you're a government agency or a private-industry corporation," he says. "Computers don't recognize those boundaries, so our mitigation strategies need to transcend those boundaries as well. All of the players in the public and the private sectors need to put a protection model into place that can do that."

Without effective information sharing between the public and the private sectors, neither side has all the data it needs to provide the best possible protection, says William Crowell, former deputy director of the National Security Agency, current chairman of the Senior Advisory Board to The Director of National Intelligence, and a member of the Security Executive Council's Board of Advisors. "I think the private sector in general is way ahead of the public sector in understanding how to approach the threats and how to build systems that deal with them. The public-sector intelligence organizations are much more aware of the sophistication of the threats. The public sector is still focused on building its own technology instead of looking at what the private sector could bring to the party if it knew more about the threats. There are thousands of new approaches to security being developed all the time, but I think for the most part the government only knows about a few that are sometimes several years old."

WHY TODAY'S OPTIONS DON'T WORK

There already exist several information-sharing forums that are intended to break down the communication barrier between public and private. This is one of the goals of United States Computer Emergency Readiness Team (US-CERT), which aims to facilitate collaboration with state and local government, industry, and international partners. There are also other CERTs and multiple Information Sharing and Analysis Centers (ISACs) for individual industries that effectively share industry-specific information, and the National Infrastructure Protection Plan has created an information-sharing environment (ISE) for 18 critical infrastructure and key resources (CIKR) sectors.

But the common call for partnership and sharing makes clear that these forums aren't working as well or as broadly as legislators would like. Both public and private entities face major obstacles to sharing.

Public-sector officials can't share sensitive information because of its sensitivity. (ISC)^2's Tipton says, "When so much information is treated as classified, we just can't get the collaboration we need. [Federal officials] may tell you, but only on a need to know. That means there's not much sharing of technology or ideas and there's no integration between what goes on in government and private sector."

Many private-sector organizations face legal obstacles to information sharing. "The Sherman antitrust act limits how much organizations who compete with each other can share," says Crowell. "That one has been an issue in several of the private sectors, particularly financial. There have also been restraints imposed by the Freedom of Information Act, which says if a private organization gives information to the government, the government gets to decide whether the information gets released to the public. That poses some really difficult problems for much of private industry, because company confidential information and brand-damaging information could be released."

In addition, many small and medium-sized businesses don't even understand why they should be part of the conversation at all. "Many small and medium businesses I've spoken to don't think they're really at risk," says Payton. "I have to explain that they could be used as part of a botnet, and that if they store credit card information from customers or social security numbers of employees, that's valuable data to attackers."

In 2009, Symantec released the results of its Storage and Security in SMBs survey, which found that globally, high numbers of small and medium businesses hadn't even taken basic precautions, such as implementing antivirus software and backing up their data.[4] "Small and large companies need to recognize that cyber attacks are a constant threat and are many times conducted by foreign government intelligence agencies," says Lynn Mattice. "Unless companies deploy sophisticated detection software, they don't realize they have lost trade secrets as a result of these attacks because they still have their information; it has simply been copied and sent back to be utilized by foreign competitors."

"Another challenge for small businesses is that they can't afford a CIO," says Payton. "They think since they're not in the tech business, it doesn't need to be a big concern. And I tell them, if you're in business, tech is your business. Because if you use a PC or keep any electronic records, you need to understand your threats and vulnerabilities. If you can't afford your own IT person, you should hire somebody to come in periodically and do a threat and vulnerability assessment. They can create a mitigation plan and train your staff on how to protect your company's information and what needs to be done to protect your infrastructure."

AN UNCERTAIN FUTURE

It's still unclear what will ultimately be done to improve public-private information sharing. The Comprehensive National Cybersecurity Initiative (CNCI), which has goals "to establish a front line of defense against today's immediate threats, defend against the full spectrum of

---

[4]"Small and Midsized Businesses Aware of Security Risks, But Not Doing All They Can to Protect Information," Symantec Corporation press release, on the Symantec website, April 9, 2009, http://www.symantec.com/about/news/release/article.jsp?prid=20090409_01, accessed April 30, 2014.

threats, and strengthen the future cybersecurity environment," is a step in the right direction.[5]

Whatever happens, says Payton, we must work to ensure that information is not only shared, but usable. "When we build this bridge of collaboration, we have to figure out how we're going to filter all this shared data into actionable information for the public and private sector," she says. "I believe there should be several avenues of communication and several forums that the private sector can use to network and collaborate with the public sector. There may be some groups or councils that need to be vertically focused for specific industries. In addition, emergency alerts regarding cyber threats need multiple levels of notification based on the level of alert. We need to facilitate bidirectional sharing between the government and private industry of core best practices and emerging threats. A combination of web conferences, in-person meetings and white papers are different approaches to get that information shared in a way that is meaningful and actionable. It's really about sitting down, negotiating what works by industry verticals and thinking through an appropriate communication plan."

START BY DOING YOUR PART

In the meantime, there are some steps private businesses can take to enhance their own cybersecurity and information-sharing efforts. Informal sharing is one underrated option, says Louis Magnotti. "There are plenty of organizations out there that foster networking among CISOs. The Security Executive Council, (ISC)^2, ISSA—these types of organizations allow CISOs to not only get to know each other but to share their mitigation strategies."

There are also private service companies that provide threat intelligence to their clients, most of whom are very large financial and retail organizations. Crowell, who is associated with one such organization, iSight Partners, says that these companies tend to remove all identifying information from the threat information they discover and then share that information with their entire customer base, creating a sort of paid information-sharing network.

---

[5]"The Comprehensive National Cybersecurity Initiative," The White House, accessed March 25, 2014, http://www.whitehouse.gov/issues/foreign-policy/cybersecurity/national-initiative.

Organizations that aren't already sharing threat information through CERT and applicable ISACs should consider doing so and should weigh the potential benefits against the perceived risks.

Businesses large and small should be ready, says Payton. "You want to have a plan that encompasses three critical areas: protect, defend, and recover. You want to make sure you have excellent defenses. However, you should also accept that, more than likely, somebody's going to get in, so you need to have an offensive strategy and a recovery strategy as well."

And more than anything else, we must not allow the increased media attention on cybersecurity to spur a backlash attitude that says the problem isn't really as big as it seems. This threat is very real, says Crowell. "Right now a lot of the attacks are what I would call reconnaissance. They could easily do significant damage, and at a critical moment that damage would have serious effects on our national security and economic situation."

CHAPTER 13

Understanding the FRCP's eDiscovery Rules

By William Plante, director of professional services for Aronson Security Group, based in Seattle.

In 1996, I was involved in a lawsuit between my then-employer and another company. My employer had engaged outside counsel for the litigation, and I needed to send some documents their way. I thought e-mail would be the best method, so I called the outside counsel to ask for an appropriate e-mail address. To my bemusement, he replied, "We don't have e-mail here," and went on to explain that his office applications were a couple of versions behind. Hiding my surprise, I pointed out that perhaps his firm was a little behind the times and at some disadvantage. The lawyer replied, "We lawyers are a bit slow to catch up, but we always manage to."

Indeed, the legal system has caught up with the information age with the amendments to the Federal Rules of Civil Procedure (FRCP) that became effective December 1, 2006. The rules, often referred to as eDiscovery, address corporate electronically stored information (ESI) that may be subpoenaed under a civil action. The rules intend to redress both real and perceived problems involving ESI.

SECURITY'S ROLE REGARDING ELECTRONICALLY STORED INFORMATION

While it is the primary domain of lawyers to take charge of legal matters, security executives should understand the principle points of the new rules and help lead necessary ESI change management within their corporations. Failing to abide by the new rules could lead to litigation sanctions that include fines, evidentiary exclusions, adverse jury instructions, increases in settlement/risk value of cases, and potential obstruction of justice and criminal liability charges.

eDiscovery rules significantly affect the way in which counsel approaches the timing and scope of discovery, the process of locating and searching data for use in legal action. The rules also place new requirements on corporate IT resources to identify, describe, preserve, and produce corporate information. Companies should reexamine their information retention program and develop a defensible strategy that includes abiding by the rules. Security leaders must become cognizant of the company's IT infrastructure and data archiving policy and programs, for data stored outside as well as within the United States.

The FRCP was amended to address seven principle areas. Let's briefly examine two of the more problematic and significant changes: Early Attention (Rule 26f) and Forms of Production (Rule 34).

RULES FOR DEALING WITH DATA

The amendments require parties to meet early in the discovery process and address ESI issues that can include preservation, scope of discovery, costs and burdens, forms of production, privilege concerns, privacy/ security/confidentiality, and accessibility. For the first time, parties are *required* to discuss ESI preservation and develop a discovery plan.

For example, many companies use third-party software to record and manage security incidents and investigation files. Upon request for discovery, how will that ESI be produced? In hard copy? Fine, but how will requests for the original source data be handled? True, the data is often in an open-architecture file format and may be accessed in a non-proprietary application. But then, how will redacted data be managed? If the data needs to be presented in court in the application in which it was originally created, does your company need to establish and maintain a legacy application library?

Data is becoming more prevalent across the enterprise in an increasing variety of forms: in e-mail, voice mail, and instant message; and on PDAs, local drives, shared drives, and websites. Preparing for litigation implies that all of these new data repositories must be included in a data and records retention policy and program. Security executives involved in litigation could be called upon to describe their company's records retention policy and be knowledgeable of the systems used to manage their department's data. Lacking a credible program or failing to adhere to the policy is indefensible in court and may expose the company to legal risk.

There is good news for security executives. At times it may simply be too onerous and burdensome for a company to track down every instance of discoverable data. The rules recognize this and permit a process to request a limit to ESI discovery. However, the respondent must identify what information it is not able to provide, explain to both the court and the plaintiff why it cannot comply, and provide sufficient detail for the court to evaluate costs and the likelihood of finding responsive data.

For example, how would a company that had purchased the intellectual assets of another company handle uncataloged ESI archived data now stored in a third-party facility? This situation is not uncommon. The costs to discover that information may be transferred from the respondent to the plaintiff in some cases. So in their own litigation planning process, plaintiffs will need to be prepared to pay for a respondent's production. Note that while the data may not be responsive, it must still be preserved.

HOW TO TAKE ACTION

You can help your organization comply with these new rules by taking the following steps:

- Know where your ESI is on a global basis including data mapping, formats, local and off-site locations, media, archiving rules, and retention policies.
- Be prepared to preserve all relevant information when a civil action is reasonably foreseeable.
- Know what data is reasonably accessible, what is not, and why.
- Know the cost to produce all data regardless of accessibility.
- Consider whether presenting legacy data will require legacy applications.
- The ability to argue information inaccessibility is related to costs and burden, so know your numbers.
- Know how you will redact privileged ESI data beforehand.

Despite all of our best efforts, discoverable and responsive data can be innocently lost. To avoid an accusation of evidence spoliation, ensure that your department adheres to the company's legal hold policy and keep your legal department informed of electronic discovery problems in a timely manner.

And it wouldn't hurt to discuss ESI with your general counsel over a coffee.

About the Contributing Editor

Bob Fahy is currently the director of corporate security at Kraft Foods. He is a seasoned multidiscipline executive security management professional with over 20 years of varied international experience in conducting and managing complex investigations; assessing threats and exposures; designing cost-effective countermeasures to mitigate threats; obtaining stakeholder consensus; and implementing appropriate asset protection programs to include but not limited to information protection, food defense, supply chain, facilities, investigations, people situational awareness, brand protection, strategic risk profiles, kidnapping, and extortion.

His broad experience in multicultural, multithreat, and multilingual environments provides unique skills in formulating policies and procedures, developing effective crisis management plans, obtaining valuable strategic and tactical threat information, and directing international complex financial fraud investigations on behalf of global stakeholders.

Bob is widely known as an energetic team player and objective communicator with a history of aligning the security group and programs with the clients' global and regional objectives.

About Elsevier's Security Executive Council Risk Management Portfolio

Elsevier's Security Executive Council Risk Management Portfolio is the voice of the security leader. It equips executives, practitioners, and educators with research-based, proven information and practical solutions for successful security and risk management programs. This portfolio covers topics in the areas of risk mitigation and assessment, ideation and implementation, and professional development. It brings trusted operational research, risk management advice, tactics, and tools to business professionals. Previously available only to the Security Executive Council community, this content—covering corporate security, enterprise crisis management, global IT security, and more—provides real-world solutions and "how-to" applications. This portfolio enables business and security executives, security practitioners, and educators to implement new physical and digital risk management strategies and build successful security and risk management programs.

Elsevier's Security Executive Council Risk Management Portfolio is a key part of the **Elsevier Risk Management & Security Collection**. The collection provides a complete portfolio of titles for the business executive, practitioner, and educator by bringing together the best imprints in risk management, security leadership, digital forensics, IT security, physical security, homeland security, and emergency management: Syngress, which provides cutting-edge computer and information security material; Butterworth-Heinemann, the premier security, risk management, homeland security, and disaster-preparedness publisher; and Anderson Publishing, a leader in criminal justice publishing for more than 40 years. These imprints, along with the addition of Security Executive Council content, bring the work of highly regarded authors into one prestigious, complete collection.

The Security Executive Council (www.securityexecutivecouncil.com) is a leading problem-solving research and services organization focused on helping businesses build value while improving their ability to effectively manage and mitigate risk. Drawing on the collective knowledge of a large community of successful security practitioners, experts, and strategic alliance partners, the Council develops strategy and insight and identifies proven practices that cannot be found anywhere else. Their research, services, and tools are focused on protecting people, brand, information, physical assets, and the bottom line.

Elsevier (www.elsevier.com) is an international multimedia publishing company that provides world-class information and innovative solutions tools. It is part of Reed Elsevier, a world-leading provider of professional information solutions in the science, medical, risk, legal, and business sectors.

Printed and bound by CPI Group (UK) Ltd, Croydon, CR0 4YY

03/10/2024

01040426-0004